GIVING OF YOURSELF AS JESUS DID

by Randy Southern

Published by Cook Ministry Resources
a division of Cook Communications Ministries

4050 Lee Vance View
Colorado Springs, Colorado 80918

Colorado Springs, CO/Paris, Ontario
www.cookministries.com
Printed in U.S.A.

Author: Randy Southern
Designer: Rebekah Lyon
Editorial Team: Cheryl Crews, Matthew Eckmann, Janna Jones, Gary Wilde, Gayle Wise, Vicki Witte

TABLE OF CONTENTS

WHY DISCIPLESHIP?

Discipleship is a well-worn word. It's been used to justify everything from programs to events. But have you ever wondered what was in the mind of God when He invented the whole concept? His infinite wisdom could have created any method to accomplish His purpose in our lives. But this all-wise God simply told us to "make disciples."

Though there are many definitions for it, we could all agree that discipleship includes the process of learning and following Christ. And the bottom line is to become like Jesus, right? As Christians, we talk a lot about doing and not enough about being (God made us human beings, not human "doings"). He desires us to be conformed to the image of His Son (Romans 8:29). That process begins at salvation and continues until we arrive on heaven's shore.

So why disciple teenagers? Why not another program or "instant growth" gimmick? Why not entertainment or the newest ministry fad? Why discipleship?

First, because students need it. Pick up your newspaper or take a walk through the halls of your local high school if you need motivation. Second, Jesus commanded and modeled it. And third, history confirms it. Put simply, it works. It avoids the prevalent quick-fix, "decision" mentality and focuses instead on a long-term lifestyle. Discipleship is not a program. It's God's plan. It involves sharing with your students both the Word and your life, which leaves a lasting impact (1 Thessalonians 2:7-8).

Discipling teenagers doesn't require that they be good-looking, intelligent, well-balanced or popular (think of the original dozen in Jesus' group!). It only requires students who are faithful learners and willing followers of Christ.

Some might say teenagers aren't ready for discipleship, that they can't handle the meat of the Word or the challenge of following Christ. Theirs is sort of a "junior Christianity." They don't have what it takes to become great for God. But we know better, don't we? So did Joseph, David, Daniel, Shadrach, Meshach, Abednego, Mary, and John Mark.

So does God.

The original Twelve disciples weren't much when they began, but they changed the course of human history. If we only had the first part of their story, we wouldn't hold out much hope for them—knowing their frequent faults and failures. But you know the rest of the story. The same is true for your students. The rest of their story is yet to be written. That's where you come in. This book is actually divided into two parts: Part One is contained in the following pages. But Part Two is yet to be written—and God has given you the opportunity to be part of writing that story as you touch your students' hearts with your life day by day.

This world desperately needs Christian youth to rise up and to answer the call of Christ to "come follow Me." This book will help them do that.

So pour your life into them. Impart the Word to them. Believe in them. Don't give up on them. Disciple them. And most of all,

Enjoy the journey!
Jeff Kinley

WHY CUSTOM DISCIPLESHIP?

So, you're convinced that what your students need is discipleship. So, why *Custom Discipleship*? Because *Custom Discipleship* acknowledges and deals with the two seemingly contradictory but central truths of discipleship.

1. There are Biblical principles that remain constant for all disciples of Jesus.
Custom Discipleship teaches students about the life of Christ and the example He set for Christians. Those stories are unchanging. The truths that Jesus communicated through word and example are the principles by which all Christians can truly live.

2. Discipleship is a dynamic, ever-changing process.
Custom Discipleship provides options that allow you to customize the learning process to meet the needs of the students in your group—no matter where they are in their relationship with Christ. This ability to customize the material keeps it dynamic and relevant to the lives of your students. Each lesson also contains *Learner Links* and *Making it Real* discipleship tips to help small-group leaders learn to share their lives with students and to grow alongside the students they are leading.

Custom Discipleship is a curriculum designed to blend the power of these truths. Let it help you as you take the challenge to disciple youth and obey Christ's command to make disciples.

Jeff Kinley is a veteran student minister, dedicated to students, parents, and youthworkers as a life calling. He is the author of several successful books, including No Turning Back, Never the Same *and* Done Deal, *(David C. Cook Church Resources). A gifted communicator, Jeff is a frequent speaker at conferences and youth camps. Jeff and his wife Beverly, have three sons—Clayton, Stuart and Davis.*

KEY QUESTIONS are the focus of the lesson. Students should be able to answer these by the end of the session.

BIBLE BASE gives the scripture references that are the basis for the whole session.

THE OPENER is optional to the session. It is a great way to get kids involved before diving into the study.

SESSION 3

WHAT A SERVANT FEELS

Key Questions
- How do our own painful experiences equip us to help others who are hurting?
- What kind of an example did Jesus set when it came to empathizing with people who are hurting?
- How can you empathize with hurting people?

Bible Base
Matthew 25:31-46
John 11:1-44
Romans 12:15

Supplies
- Flip chart
- Pens
- Pencils or pens
- Index cards
- Copies of Resources 3A, 3B, and Journal

Opener [Optional]

Common Ground
Ask your students to pull their chairs into a circle. Choose one of your group members to start the game standing in the middle of the circle. Remove his or her chair from the circle (think Musical Chairs). The person in the middle will call out a category. The category may be anything from "Collects comic books" to "Born in another state" to "Hates country music." Everyone in the group who fits the category must stand up and run to an empty seat. The person in the middle, meanwhile, must also try to get to an open chair. The person who doesn't make it must then stand in the middle of the circle and call out the next category.

LEARNER LINK
This Link activity is designed to stretch your students' brains a bit. Many of the answers on Resource 3A may sound very close to correct but are not the best answers. Watch to see how deeply your students struggle with the issue of suffering. This question has been asked through the centuries, and there is no easy answer.

This activity may prove to be an effective bonding exercise for your group members. They may be surprised to find out that other people in the group share their interests, experiences, or background.

MAKING IT REAL
As you get to know your students better, pray for them specifically. Taking the time to do this will help you to focus on their needs. It will also help you to continually acknowledge and trust that it is God who is making these kids into disciples of Jesus Christ—sometimes even in spite of your efforts!

CUSTOM DISCIPLESHIP 33

SUPPLIES listed here are those needed for the core lesson. Any supplies for options are listed with that optional activity.

BOLD TYPE signifies "teacher talk"—things to be said directly by the leader of the group.

THERE ARE THREE LINKS that divide each session, taking students through the learning process and into personal application.

LEARNER LINKS are located through the sessions to give the leader extra tips on how to help their students learn the Word of God.

MAKING IT REAL sections are tips on discipleship located throughout the sessions.

After your group members have weighed in on the topic of Jesus' empathy, ask: Maybe one of the reasons God allows us to experience pain, suffering, loss, and hard times is so that we will be better able to understand what other hurting people are going through and be better prepared to help them? Why or why not? Let your group members offer their opinions.

Link 3

Empathy 'n' Me
Ask: Have you ever had someone say to you, "I know just how you're feeling"? If so, how did you feel when you heard those words? Did you believe the person? Why or why not? These words are especially popular at funerals. Usually the people who use the phrase don't mean any disrespect by it; they just might not know what else to say.

What if the person really did know how you feel—somewhat, at least? What if he or she had gone through a similar experience? Would you be interested in talking to that person? Why?

After a few students have offered their thoughts, say: Okay, let's reverse the situation. Let's say you run into someone who's hurting or in need of help. Let's say that the person is going through a situation similar to one you went through a year or so ago. Would you be interested in talking to that person? If some of your group members express reluctance, listen to their reasons for not getting involved. Invite the rest of the group to respond to those reasons.

The resource sheet "What I've Got to Give" (Resource 3B) is designed to help your group members identify the things in their lives that qualify them to be truly empathetic, the situations and circumstances they've experienced that make them experts of sorts in dealing with specific kinds of hurt.

Encourage your students to take this assignment seriously. Emphasize that no one will be asked to share anything on the sheet that he or she is uncomfortable with.

LEARNER LINK
If any of your group members are brave enough to share their responses to Resource 3B, you will need to respect their feelings, as well as their privacy. You may need to ask a few questions to clarify a point or to correct a possible misunderstanding, but try not to pry for more information. Do not put your students in a position where they feel pressure to reveal more than they want to. When your volunteers finish sharing, be quick to affirm them, and encourage the rest of the group to do the same.

After a few minutes, ask if there are any volunteers who would like to share some of the things they wrote down. After the volunteers have shared, discuss as a group the possibility that there are people in this world who can benefit from the negative things that have happened to us.

MAKING IT REAL
A big part of discipleship is encouraging your students to put what they have learned into action. As their leader, you should be constantly looking for teachable moments—times when you are together with the students, outside of your group time, in which you can encourage them to practice what they have been learning. Another great way to do this is to set up service projects or experiential learning times. Session five in this book provides what you need to set up one of these learning experiences.

Before you wrap up this session, throw out a few more questions to the group: What if you run into someone who's facing a problem you've never encountered? Let's say you've never had any experience with this kind of problem. Can you still offer that person empathy? If so, how?

34 CUSTOM DISCIPLESHIP

OPTION ICONS are located at the beginning of each link to let you know that there are options for those groups at the end of the session.

RESOURCE PAGES are noted throughout the session. The actual pages are reproducible and can be found at the end of each session.

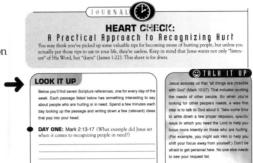

LOOK IT UP! is a section of the student journal page that encourages kids to continue their process of discipleship through the week. It provides a passage of Scripture and a question for each day of the week.

TALK IT UP! provides a place to write down personal prayer requests as well as the needs of accountability partners.

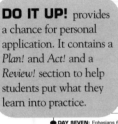

DO IT UP! provides a chance for personal application. It contains a *Plan!* and *Act!* and a *Review!* section to help students put what they learn into practice.

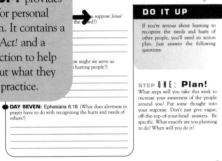

CHECKLIST of options allows you to keep track of which options you have used.

OPTIONS are designed for specific types of groups but provide great variety if you want to mix and match.

EACH ICON represents a type of group and designates options specific for that group.

THIS HEADING tells the section of the session where this option can be used.

1

WHAT A
SERVANT SEES

Key Questions
- How did Jesus recognize the needs of others?
- What kind of an example did Jesus set when He met the needs of others?
- How will you recognize the needy and hurting people around you?

Bible Base
Mark 5:24b-34

Supplies
- Copies of Resources 1A, 1B, and Journal
- Pencils or pens

Opener (Optional)

Finders

Kick off this unit with a game that doubles as both an icebreaker and a competition. Before the session, you'll need to spend a few minutes talking to your group members individually. Your goal is to discover one or more obscure pieces of information about each person—things that few, if any, of the other group members know. You're not looking for extremely personal stuff here, just some interesting tidbits, like finding someone who was named after a famous actress, or, someone who fell asleep on the living room floor last night—and stayed there all night.

The game itself is simple. You'll read the tidbits one at a time and group members will try to find the person who fits that description. The first person to find someone fitting a description gets a point. The person with the most points at the end of the game is the winner. What you don't want to do is give your students any instructions for finding the people in question. Let them come up with their own fact-finding strategies and techniques.

MAKING IT R E A L

For the next four or five weeks, you will be teaching your students what it means to be a disciple of Jesus Christ. One of the most helpful things you can do to help them grow as disciples is to assign "accountability partners." Explain to your group members that for the next few weeks, accountability partners will be responsible for checking on and encouraging each other's growth as disciples. The partners should plan on hooking up at least twice a week (whether at school or by phone) to update each other on their discipleship efforts.

After everyone has been "found," talk about how easy or difficult it was to locate the person (or persons) who fit each description. Some students may have been easy to spot because of the look on their face when they were described. Others may have been more inscrutable. If no one else mentions it, point out that the three most valuable qualities for succeeding in the game were (1) a natural curiosity about people, (2) an observant eye, and (3) a willingness to talk to others.

Link 1

What Do You See?

Hand out copies of "I Spy" (Resource 1A). Make sure, though, that all of the sheets are facedown when you distribute them. Don't let group members turn the sheets over until you give the signal. When you say **Go**, your students will have 30 seconds to study the page carefully, trying to remember everything they can about what's on it. When you call **Time**, they must turn their sheets back over and not look at the objects anymore.

Ask some questions about the sheet to see how observant your students are. You can get as detailed as you like with the questions, but try to focus on elements of the sheet that your group members may have overlooked. Here are some sample questions to get you started:
• **What was the object in the bottom-right corner of the page?**
• **What object was immediately to the left of the apple?**
• **How many eggs were in the nest?**

Briefly talk about how difficult it was to pick out the details of the sheet in such a short time. Then ask: **How good are you at spotting details in everyday life?** Encourage your group members to rate themselves on a scale of one to ten. Discuss what it takes to be a good "detail person."

Then ask: **What things do you miss during the course of a day because you're not paying attention?** If no one else mentions it, ask: **Do you sometimes miss the hurts and needs in other people's lives? Why?**

Link 2

The Needs around Jesus

What needs did the people around Jesus have? There will probably be the "standard" answer about the physical needs. If so, ask: **What other needs that were not easily seen on the surface did those people have?**

Say: **Obviously Jesus was God's Son so He knew about everyone's needs before any of them ever spoke. In fact, there is one example of a woman that Jesus healed before she even said a word. But Jesus knew.** Have someone read Mark 5:24b-34.

To set the stage, in this story, we catch up with Jesus when His public ministry was really taking off by showing God's power through healing people and casting out demons. Here, Jesus was actually on His way to bring a man's daughter back to life. Needless to say, scores of people wanted to be in on this miracle.

Ask: **Jesus was the most popular man at that moment. All eyes were on Him. That hardly seems the ideal place for a woman who was cast out from society to be—right there, in the midst of everybody, elbowing her way to Jesus.**

Now ask your students to switch their attention in this story to the woman. Ask: **What do we know about her from the passage?** (She was out of money, outcast from society because she was "unclean," she was desperate for healing, etc.) Ask a volunteer to make a list of the things the other group members say. Once the group runs out of things they can surmise from the story, have the volunteer read the list back to the group.

Then say, **One word we could use to describe her could be "outcast." How do we know? Portions of Jewish law from the Old Testament said God's people were to be very careful not to come in contact with someone who was bleeding. That meant that this woman spent many years of her life without friends and alone. And although the Bible never tells us exactly what was wrong with this woman, it is clear that she must have suffered greatly, not just physically, but emotionally, financially, and socially.**

LEARNER LINK

The optional opener dealt with three qualities that Jesus demonstrated here: a natural curiosity about people, an observant eye, and a willingness to talk to others. Discuss briefly how these qualities might come in handy for someone trying to spot other people's hurts.

Perhaps the most curious part of the story is not necessarily her healing, though. Ask your students to split into two groups and reread verses 30-34. Have them come up with what they think is the reason why Jesus made such a big deal out of this woman touching His clothes.

After three or four minutes have each group give an answer. Then discuss: **Jesus didn't allow that woman to shrink away, healed. How was her physical life different after touching Jesus? How was her emotional life different after Jesus called attention to her?** Make sure your students understand that, because Jesus made a big deal out of her healing, He also restored her standing socially; she was no longer considered an outcast and "unclean." Jesus demonstrated that He was just as concerned about her emotional healing as her physical.

Link 3

See the Hurt

Hand out copies of "Hidden Hurts" (Resource 1B). Have students stay in their two groups to complete the sheet. After a few minutes, ask volunteers from the groups to share some of the hurts they recognized in the people on the sheet. Use the following information and questions to supplement your discussion of the sheet.

Luanne
Luanne's life will be changed forever by her parents' divorce. Though we don't know the specifics of Luanne's family life, it's probably safe to say that Luanne's confidence has been shaken. After all, if a 19-year marriage isn't secure, what is?

Ask: **If you didn't know anything about Luanne's situation at home, what might you think of her if you ran into her in the hall?** If she ignored you in the hall, you might think she was a snob. Or you might think you had unknowingly done something to make her mad.

Evan
Sometimes a move is almost as devastating as a death. Both result in separation. Evan seems to have been devastated by the loss of his friend. He's also probably struggling with identity issues, trying to figure out who he is and what "role" he wants to play in school.

Ask: **What would you think if you saw Evan sitting in the back of the class, not saying anything to anybody?** You might think he was stuck up, or lonely. **How would you know the truth about Evan?** Lonely people are often insecure and waiting for someone to talk to them first.

Reese

Imagine the humiliation Reese must feel. The mistakes of the mother have come back to haunt the daughter. Reese's shame and loss of confidence in her mother are hard enough to deal with. Throw in the taunting of classmates, and you've got the makings of a horrible situation.

Ask: **If you knew nothing about Reese and merely overheard the comment in the lunchroom, what would you have thought of her? What would you see in Reese if you looked beyond what you know of her family background?**

Rod

It's likely that behind Rod's mask of hostility is a very frightened and hurt young man. Often when people lash out at others, it's a preemptive strike—"doing unto others *before* they do unto you." Usually that kind of behavior is the result of feeling neglected or rejected at home. It's a good guess that Rod has problems with his self-esteem and that he's uncomfortable in social situations. It's also a good guess that what he needs more than anything are friends, the very things that his personality keeps him from having.

Ask: **If you were to look at Rod strictly on the surface, what would you see? What would it take for you to be able to see beneath Rod's obnoxious surface, to get a glimpse of the hurt in his life?**

Do any of the people on the sheet seem familiar to you? Do you know anyone with similar personalities or character traits? Encourage your group members to describe—without naming names—people they know who are reminiscent of Luanne, Evan, Reese, or Rod.

Have you ever thought about what goes on inside these people—what makes them the way they are? If you have, what conclusions did you come to? Ask group members to share—again, without naming names—some of the thoughts they've had about the motivating factors in people's lives. Encourage other group members to offer their opinions, based on the descriptions.

Think about the factors surrounding the life of the woman Jesus healed. Jesus knew she was hurting physically and emotionally. Jesus restored her and offered her a place with other people. What about you? If you're not the type of person who naturally thinks about other people's hurts, how might the example of Jesus help you become that type of person?

LEARNER LINK

It will be helpful for each one of your students to have a discipleship notebook. You can create these using three-ring binders or simple file folders. (If your folders are the standard 8.5 x 11 you will need to copy the resource pages at 120%.) Encourage your students to keep all of the resource pages that they receive in this notebook. This will be especially helpful as they work through the daily readings and questions for the "Heart Check" pages. You may also want to provide some extra paper for them to use as journal pages. The whole purpose of this is to help your students see discipleship as an ongoing process and to help them continue to grow outside of the group.

MAKING IT R E A L

Encourage your students to share prayer requests with each other. You may want to have a specific time to do this as a group or encourage accountability partners to do that sometime during the week. Ask students to commit to praying for those requests. Encourage your students to include requests related to this session, including asking God to help the group members recognize the needs in the people around them.

This is more of a get-your-group-members-thinking type of question than a find-the-right-answer type. Your goal here is to have your students thinking about recognizing other people's hurts when they walk out the door. As a group, spend a minute or two throwing out suggestions for ways to live out the three things Jesus showed: a natural curiosity about people, an observant eye, and a willingness to talk to others.

Ask your students to get with their accountability partners. Hand out copies of the student sheet, "Heart Check: A Practical Approach to Recognizing Hurt" (Resource 1C). Have each student look at the "Do it Up" section and fill out the plan for what he or she will do this week to notice the needs around him or her. If some accountability pairs finish before others, encourage them to share things that they can pray about for each other during the week. Close in prayer as a group.

I Spy

Take a look at these. What do you see? How much will you remember?

All photo images © PhotoDisc, Inc.

© PhotoDisc, Inc.

Hidden Hurts

Because hurts come in all shapes and sizes, they're not always easy to spot. Sometimes you have to look beyond the surface to get a glimpse of them. Below you'll find descriptions of four people. Read each description, and write down some of the hurts you think that person might be feeling.

Luanne

Luanne hasn't been herself lately. Not that you know her really well or anything. You see her occasionally at church and in the halls at school, but since she's a year older than you, you're not in the same social circle. Usually, though, when she sees you, she smiles and says hi. For the past couple of weeks, she's stopped doing that. You thought she was just developing an attitude until you overheard your mother on the phone talking about what a shame it was that Luanne's parents were divorcing after 19 years of marriage.

_____

_____

_____

Rod

Most people would agree that Rod's only purpose in life seems to be making fun of everyone and everything he can. This guy is a nonstop insult machine. Most people respond to Rod's verbal assaults in one of three ways. Some, primarily freshman guys, laugh wildly at his insults, perhaps hoping to spare themselves from his attacks. Others, usually upperclassmen and football players, resort to threats of physical violence—which generally manage to shut Rod up for a minute or two. The rest simply ignore him, dismissing his insults with a heartfelt, "Shut up, loser." As you might have guessed, aside from his small band of freshman groupies, Rod has very few friends.

_____

_____

_____

Evan

If you were in a class with Evan and David, you knew you were going to have fun. Everybody loved them, students and teachers alike. They were just hilarious when they were together. It's like they were a comedy team or something. You rarely saw one of them without the other. They were always either laughing themselves or making others laugh. At the end of last school year, though, David's family moved away. Now Evan is on his own. People still expect him to be funny, but his heart's just not in it. He rarely says anything in class anymore. He just keeps to himself, seemingly out of place in the hallways he once owned.

_____

_____

_____

Reese

You're standing next to a girl named Reese in the lunch line, waiting to pay for your food, when you hear all kinds of whispering and snickering going on around you. Someone yells to the cashier, "Make sure she pays in cash!" and six or seven people burst out laughing. Reese mutters something obscene under her breath, pays for her food, and hurries away. You're not sure what's going on, so the person next to you fills you in. "Reese's mom got arrested for writing bad checks last week. Her name was in the paper and everything."

_____

_____

_____

HEART CHECK:
A Practical Approach to Recognizing Hurt

You may think you've picked up some valuable tips for becoming aware of hurting people, but unless you actually put those tips to use in your life, they're useless. Keep in mind that Jesus wants not only "listeners" of His Word, but "doers" (James 1:22). This sheet is for doers.

LOOK IT UP

Below you'll find seven Scripture references, one for every day of the week. Each passage listed below has something interesting to say about people who are hurting or in need. Spend a few minutes each day looking up the passage and writing down a few (relevant) ideas that pop into your head.

DAY ONE: Mark 2:13-17 (What example did Jesus set when it comes to recognizing people in need?)

_____
_____
_____
_____

DAY TWO: Ephesians 5:1-2 (How would an imitator of God respond to hurting people?)

_____
_____
_____
_____

DAY THREE: Romans 5:6-8 (What is the most important need the Lord recognized in us?)

_____
_____
_____
_____

DAY FOUR: 2 Corinthians 1:3-4 (Why does God comfort us?)

_____
_____
_____
_____

☺ TALK IT UP

Jesus assures us that "all things are possible with God" (Mark 10:27). That includes spotting the needs of other people. So when you're looking for other people's needs, a wise first step is to talk to God about it. Take some time to write down a few prayer requests, specific ways in which you need the Lord to help you focus more intently on those who are hurting. (For example, you might ask Him to help you shift your focus away from yourself.) Don't be afraid to get personal here. No one else needs to see your request list.

_____
_____
_____
_____
_____
_____
_____
_____
_____
_____
_____
_____
_____
_____
_____
_____

DAY FIVE: Mark 6:35-43 (How do you suppose Jesus' disciples recognized the need of the crowd?)

_____
_____
_____
_____

DAY SIX: Psalm 119:50 (How might we serve as ambassadors of God's comfort to hurting people?)

_____
_____
_____
_____

DAY SEVEN: Ephesians 6:18 (What does alertness in prayer have to do with recognizing the hurts and needs of others?)

_____
_____
_____
_____

DO IT UP

If you're serious about learning to recognize the needs and hurts of other people, you'll need an action plan. Just answer the following questions.

STEP ONE: Plan!

What steps will you take this week to increase your awareness of the people around you? Put some thought into your response. Don't just give vague, off-the-top-of-your-head answers. Be specific. What exactly are you planning to do? When will you do it?

STEP TWO: Do!

If you did take some steps to increase your awareness of other people's needs and hurts, did things progress as you thought they would? Was shifting your focus outward easier or harder than you expected? How much has your need-spotting improved?

STEP THREE: Review!

Do you believe Jesus is proud of your efforts to shift your focus to the needs of others? Do you feel any different toward people in need now? Do you think anyone else has recognized your shift in focus?

LITTLE BIBLE BACKGROUND

Link 2

If your students have trouble picturing the Son of God, Jesus, as a flesh-and-blood person, review a few Scripture passages that illustrate His humanity. He was conceived supernaturally apart from any human father, but He was born naturally of a human mother (Matt. 1:18). He grew like a normal child, both physically and mentally (Luke 2:40). He experienced hunger (Matt. 4:2) and thirst (John 19:28). He got tired after long journeys (John 4:6). He required sleep (Matt. 8:24).

Link 3

If your group members aren't familiar at all with God's Word, you may want to spend a minute or two reviewing the second-most important command in all of Scripture. Read Matthew 22:39. Ask: **Do you think it's possible to love other people as much as you love yourself? If so, how would you show that love in your day-to-day actions?** Suggest that this kind of love requires a change of priorities, from a self-centered perspective to an others-centered perspective.

ADVANCED LEARNERS

Link 1

Here's a tough challenge for your Bible know-it-alls: **Name three people in the Bible who were oblivious—either by choice or by circumstances—to the needs and hurts of people around them.** Students might suggest people like the priest and the Levite in the story of the good Samaritan, who left an injured man lying in the road while they went about their business.

Link 2

If your students are used to responding to questions that have obvious or "right" answers, cross them up with a brief soul-searching exercise. Ask: **How has Jesus met your deepest need?** Affirm anyone who has the guts to answer this tough question. The purpose of this question is to help your students understand that Jesus is always able to meet our needs.

MOSTLY GUYS

Link 2

Ask: **How important is loyalty and dependability when it comes to friendship? Have you ever let one of your friends down when they needed you? If so, what happened? How did you feel about it?** If you suspect that your guys aren't comfortable with sharing their own faults, ask: **Have you ever been let down by a friend? If so, what happened? How did you feel about it?**

Link 3

Ask: **Do you believe that guys are taught, either directly or indirectly, to ignore their hurt, to "suck it up" and not whine about the things that are bothering them? If so, how might that affect the way you approach other guys who you believe are hurting?** This is an important topic to discuss. Getting past guys' natural defenses is a big part of recognizing their hurt.

MOSTLY GIRLS

Link 2

After reading Mark 5:24b-34, ask: **We all have things we try to keep inside. But most of the time, that only makes things worse. Have you had friends who, instead of like the woman in this story, kept things hidden away? What can you do to help them?**

Link 3

Ask: **Which of the people on Resource 1B would you be most reluctant to get involved with? Why?** Briefly explore your girls' comfort level when it comes to helping people who are hurting or in need.

MEDIA

Link 1

Rather than using Resource 1A, it would be great if you could make a "mini-movie" on video, something no longer than two minutes, for your group members to watch. It doesn't really matter whether your movie has a plot, or even actors, for that matter. What you want to do is load your movie with details—so many details that your students have trouble remembering them all. After you show your video to the group, ask questions to see how many of those details your students spotted.

Link 3

Bring in a video of the movie *Angus*, the story of an overweight nerd who, as a cruel joke, is voted king of his high school's winter dance. Play the scene at the end of the movie in which Angus's best friend Troy betrays him by turning over an embarrassing video of Angus to his enemies. On the night of the dance, the enemies humiliate Angus by showing the video on large monitors for the whole school to see. Discuss as a group the hurts that the different characters are feeling after the betrayal and humiliation.

EXTRA ADRENALINE

Link 1

Send students out of the room one at a time. While each person is gone, move one item (or person) in the room to a different location. When the person returns, he or she has 30 seconds to spot the out-of-place object and move it back to its original location. Use this activity to introduce the idea of being aware of the things that are going on around us.

Link 3

Ask for pairs of volunteers to act out scenarios based on the descriptions on Resource 1B. One volunteer should play the person described on the sheet; the other should play someone trying to recognize the needs or pain in that person's life during a casual conversation. Encourage your volunteers to make the roleplays as realistic as possible.

JUNIOR HIGH

Link 1

Junior highers are generally self-centered by nature. Use this fact to your advantage as you introduce the idea of recognizing people's hurts and needs. Ask: **When was the last time you were hurting inside or** in need of some kind of help, and no one seemed to notice? Start out by allowing your group members to focus on themselves. Then ask: **What can we do to keep other people from feeling the same way we did?**

Link 3
Rather than using Resource 1B, which may be beyond your younger group members, read the following scenario and ask group members to identify some needs or hurts the person may be dealing with.
• Dewayne has had trouble fitting in at your school since the day he arrived. He moved to your area in the middle of the school year, after all of the cliques had already been formed. As a result, making friends was nearly impossible for him. The fact that he usually wears dirty clothes to school makes him a big target for teasing and abuse. On top of everything else, last week the school nurse found lice in Dewayne's hair. Now no one will go within two feet of him.

Planning Checklist
LINK 1: What Do You See?
❑ Advanced Learners
❑ Media
❑ Extra Adrenaline
❑ Junior High

LINK 2: The Needs around Jesus
❑ Little Bible Background
❑ Advanced Learners
❑ Mostly Guys
❑ Mostly Girls

LINK 3: See the Hurt
❑ Little Bible Background
❑ Mostly Guys
❑ Mostly Girls
❑ Media
❑ Extra Adrenaline
❑ Junior High

2
WHAT A
SERVANT GIVES

Key Questions
- What is our responsibility to people who are hurting or in need?
- What example did Jesus set when it comes to giving what we have to help people who are hurting?
- What can you offer to people who are hurting?

Bible Base
Luke 10:25-37
Romans 5:6-11

Supplies
- Pencils or pens
- Copies of Resources 2A, 2B, and Journal

Opener (Optional)
Good Samaritan Mad-Lib

If you've never done a mad-lib before, here's how it works. You will ask your group members to supply you with different words and parts of speech. You will then plug their suggestions into the text below to create a new version of the good Samaritan story. Here is the list of requests for your group members:

The Parable of the Guy Who Had Something Happen to Him
While He Was on His Way Somewhere
(Based really, really, really loosely on Luke 10:30-35)

"A man was going down from Jerusalem to _____ , when he fell into the hands of _____ .
                                          location   occupation

They stripped him of his _____ , _____ him, and _____ away, leaving him
                          a possession   verb   verb
                          held dear   (past tense)   (past tense)

half _____ . A _____ happened to be going down the same road, and when he saw the man,
     physical condition   occupation
     (past tense)

he _____ by on the other side. So too, a _____ , when he came to the place and saw him,
   verb   nationality
   (past tense)

_____ by on the other side. But a _____ , as
verb   nationality
(past tense)

he traveled, came where the man was; and when he saw

him, he _____ _____ on him. He went to
        verb   noun
        (past tense)   (a thing)

MAKING IT REAL

Introduce your group members to the art of journaling. Ask your students to keep a journal or diary of their observations, feelings, and frustrations as they take steps each day to be a more devoted disciple of Jesus Christ. Encourage them to be consistent in writing in their journals. Point out that journaling may be difficult at first, but that the more they do it, the better they will become. Furthermore, the better they become, the more they will benefit from it.

him and bandaged his _____, pouring on _____and _____. Then he put the man on
noun
(plural)   liquid   liquid

his own _____, took him to an_____and took care of him. The next day he took out
animal   type of business

two _____ _____ and gave them to the _____. 'Look after him,'
color   noun   occupation
(plural)

he said, 'and when I return, I will _____you for any extra _____you may have.' "
verb   noun

As group members call out their suggestions, write them down in the corresponding blanks. Keep an eye on the text as you choose which suggestions to use, trying to find words that fit—in a goofy, odd kind of way. After you've filled in all of the blanks, read the story back to your group members.

Link 1

Big Help in Small Packages

If you handed out Resource 1C at the end of Session 1, take a few minutes at the beginning of this meeting to find out how well your students did at recognizing hurting people last week. Ask volunteers to share their experiences, both positive and negative, with the rest of the group. In addition, you may want to ask if anyone wrote down needs they observed in their discipleship notebooks (see Learner Link from Session 1). Encourage other group members to comment on the volunteers' experiences; ask: **How did he/she do with his/her plan?** Emphasize that you're looking for meaningful praise and suggestions. Your group members should feel comfortable enough with each other to be open and honest about their struggles and successes.

Start off your meeting with two questions: **What's the nicest thing anyone's ever done for you?** and **What's the nicest thing you've ever done for someone else?** Spend a few minutes talking about generous gestures and meaningful sacrifices.

Hand out copies of "Random Acts of Kindness" (Resource 2A). Let students work in pairs to add their ideas to the sheet. After a few minutes, ask volunteers to read some of the things they came up with.

Then ask: **How would our world be different if more people committed themselves to random acts of kindness?** Encourage your students to think big in their projections. A massive outburst of selflessness and generosity would probably have some wide-reaching effects. Then ask, **What keeps people from doing these things?**

LEARNER LINK

Let your students know that kindness is rarely ever as "random" as we think. With all the suffering in the world so outweighing kindness, it should be easy to see that we all love hearing about "random acts of kindness" but few people actually live that way.

How would your corner of the world be different if you committed yourself to random acts of kindness? After a few students have responded, announce that today's session will deal with the topic of giving unselfishly. Explain that, as followers of Jesus, your group will be looking at two of the most famous examples of unselfish giving ever recorded—one of which is a fictional story Jesus told (the good Samaritan) and the other is the real way Jesus changed the world (His sacrifice for our sins).

Link 2

Unexpected Mercy

If you used the Optional Opener, introduce the Bible study this way: **Believe it or not, the story we read earlier is not the way the parable of the good Samaritan goes. I don't want you leaving here thinking that the Samaritan transported the injured man to the nearest** *convenience store* **on a** *rhinoceros,* **so we'd better take a look at what the Bible actually does say.** (Obviously you'll need to substitute the words in italics with the actual results of your group's mad-libs.)

Have someone read Luke 10:25-37. Then ask: **What do you suppose the injured man thought when he saw the priest coming his way?** Chances are, he probably expected help. After all, if you can't count on a religious leader to help you, who can you count on?

Explain that a Levite, in this situation, would have been similar to a church deacon—a lay leader who was respected in religious circles. Ask: **If you'd been the injured man, how do you suppose you would have felt when the Levite passed by without helping?** In addition to being disappointed, you might tend to feel like an outcast, as though you're not worthy of being helped.

The passage doesn't say so, but we can assume that the injured man was Jewish. In Jesus' day, Jewish people hated Samaritans and treated them like second-class citizens. How do you suppose the injured man felt when he saw a Samaritan heading his way? He probably felt helpless and vulnerable, perhaps even expecting to be taunted or harmed further by this man whom his people considered an enemy.

What do you notice about the Samaritan in this story? How did he act? First, he took immediate action. He saw someone in need and got involved. Second, he ignored prejudices. It didn't matter to him that the injured man was Jewish, an enemy of the Samaritans. He saw only a person with a serious need. Third, his concern for the injured man was genuine and long-lasting. He made arrangements with the innkeeper to return much later to check on the man's condition and settle his bill.

On a scale of one to ten, how would you rate the Samaritan's helping skills? Ask those who respond to explain their rankings and perhaps suggest other things the Samaritan might have done.

Why do you suppose the priest and the Levite refused to help the injured man? Maybe they were late for appointments. Maybe they suspected that the man wasn't really injured but was a robber trying to catch them off guard. Maybe they just didn't want to get involved in other people's problems.

What point do you think Jesus was making when He made the Samaritan, a hated foreigner, the hero of His story? Jesus' main purpose for telling the story was to answer the man who asked, "Who is my neighbor?" Jesus' point was that our neighbors, the people we are instructed to love as ourselves, can be anyone (especially anyone in need).

Now help your students make the connection between "helping" and "sacrificing." Ask one or more of these questions before proceeding:

• What does it take to be a helper of hurting people?
• What role does giving play in helping?
• To help people, how much of ourselves will we likely have to give? Can you share an example?
• Would you say, then, that self-sacrifice is a key aspect of helping others? Explain.

Say something like this: **In Jesus' story, the good Samaritan helped by giving of himself. He sacrificed his time, his energy, and his money to help someone he didn't even know. But Jesus never just talked about** stuff like this. He also set for us an example from His own life. And Jesus' sacrifice was even more extreme. Have someone read Romans 5:6-11. Ask: **How do you feel after you hear that passage from Romans? What was so extreme about Jesus' sacrifice?**

Continue: **One thing Jesus never intended for us to do was just to sit back and watch other people suffer. Jesus, like the Samaritan, acted on behalf of other people all the time. With these two examples in front of you, what would you be willing to give in order to help people in need?** This is a rhetorical question, designed to introduce Link 3 of the session, but if your group members want to throw out a few suggestions, let them.

Link 3

What Do You Have to Give?

Spend the remaining time in this session discussing specific, practical ways in which your group members can use their time, energy, money, and other resources to help hurting or needy people. Hand out copies of "What Can I Give?" (Resource 2B). If you like, you can make this resource sheet into a sharing time by asking your students to work through the sheet with their accountability partners from the first session.

After your students have spent a few minutes answering the questions, ask for volunteers to read their answers to the questions on the sheet. As the group leader, your challenge during this small-group discussion time is to encourage your students to think as broadly as possible in answering these questions. Contribute the following information to the discussion groups, as needed.

1. Even "common" skills like being a good listener or having a natural curiosity about people can be powerful tools for meeting people's needs. How many nursing home residents do you suppose would enjoy talking with a young person who's genuinely interested in what they have to say?

2. Even a few hours a week is enough time to make a difference in the life of a child from a single-parent home. Why not be a mentor?

3. Even a few dollars a week is enough to support a child through a hunger-relief organization. What's more, if you make a commitment to set aside a few dollars a week, eventually you will have enough money for a large purchase. The key is making the initial commitment to save.

LEARNER LINK

It is true that all humans have the tremendous capability for both compassion and selfishness. And at no age is this more easily seen than high school. One of the challenges of this session is to show your students several ways they can mold their desires with the compassion of Christ. Encourage them to find ways to serve others that use their talents and skills. That is the way God has made each of them, and that's how they can succeed in helping others.

4. A car can be an extremely useful ministry resource. Perhaps there's an elderly person in your church who needs rides to and from the doctor, the grocery store, and other places. Why not do some part-time chauffeuring?

As you conclude the session, ask your students to spend a couple of minutes praying about the ways they can help other people and sacrifice this week. Then, hand out copies of the take-home sheet "Heart Check: A Practical Approach to Giving to People in Need" (Resource 2C). The sheet is intended to motivate each group member to one specific act of selfless generosity this week. Encourage your students to set aside a few minutes each day to work on the sheet and follow through on their "action plans."

MAKING IT R E A L

Some of your students may have needs that don't get addressed during your group time. Make a special effort to get to know all of your kids individually. That may mean a phone call or a trip to a sporting event or a lunch together. Not only will this help you build relationships with the students, but seeing you outside of your discipleship group will help them connect what they learn to their everyday lives.

Random Acts of Kindness

You may be surprised by how much people appreciate out-of-the-ordinary gestures and off-the-wall ways of showing you care. Here are ten such gestures. Your job is to come up with as many more as you can think of.

Photo images by ©PhotoDisc, Inc.

Send your favorite former teacher a flower arrangement, along with a note telling her what a difference she made in your life.

Make a tape of fun songs for someone who's going through tough times.

Pay a toll for the car behind you.

Name your pet after someone who's made a difference in your life.

The day before your brother or friend has a big date, wash his car for him.

The next time you're in a fast-food restaurant, buy an extra meal and give it to the first homeless person you see on the street.

Stop a total stranger in the mall to pay him or her a sincere compliment.

Make sure no one in your school cafeteria eats alone.

Sponsor a child in a Third World country.

What Can I Give?

The Good Samaritan is more than just a nice story. Jesus told this parable to challenge people to get beyond prejudice and fear, and begin to sacrifice to help those in need. Take a few minutes and answer these questions.

1. What skills, talents, or gifts do you have that could be put to use to help other people?

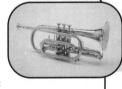

2. How much time would you be willing to devote each week to help those who are in need?

3. How much money would you be willing to set aside each week to help those who are less fortunate than you?

4. What other resources do you have that might come in handy in helping the needy?

Photo images by ©PhotoDisc, Inc.

HEART CHECK:
A Practical Approach to Giving to People in Need

You may think you've picked up some valuable tips for being unselfish and generous, but unless you actually put those tips to use in your life, they're useless. Remember, God wants not only "listeners" of His Word, but "doers" (James 1:22). This sheet is for doers.

LOOK IT UP

Below you'll find seven Scripture references, one for every day of the week. Each passage listed below has something interesting to say about giving to people in need. Spend a few minutes each day looking up the passage and writing down a few (relevant) ideas that pop into your head.

DAY ONE: 1 John 3:16-20 (What material possessions do you have that might be useful to someone in need?)

_____
_____
_____
_____

DAY TWO: Proverbs 19:17 (How does the Lord benefit when we give to the poor?)

_____
_____
_____
_____

DAY THREE: Matthew 6:1-4 (Why are we supposed to be quiet about the generous things we do?)

_____
_____
_____
_____

DAY FOUR: Matthew 5:42 (Why is it sometimes hard to lend our possessions freely?)

_____
_____
_____
_____

☺ TALK IT UP

Jesus assures us that "all things are possible with God" (Mark 10:27). That includes using your time, energy, and resources to help other people. So when you're faced with an obstacle that interferes with your commitment to people in need, a wise first step is to talk to God about it. Take some time to write down a few prayer requests, specific ways in which you need the Lord to help you focus on your responsibilities to the needy. (For example, you might ask Him to help you identify resources you have that could be useful to other people.) Don't be afraid to get personal here. No one else needs to see your request list.

_____
_____
_____
_____
_____
_____
_____
_____
_____
_____
_____
_____
_____
_____
_____
_____

DAY FIVE: John 15:12-13 (Under what conditions would you be willing to follow Jesus' example and lay down your life for someone else?)

_____

_____

_____

_____

DAY SIX: James 2:14-17 (How is faith related to works—and vice versa?)

_____

_____

_____

_____

DAY SEVEN: Matthew 25:31-46 (What is our reward for helping people in need?)

_____

_____

_____

_____

DO IT UP

If you're serious about giving what you have to help others, you'll need an action plan. Just answer the following questions.

STEP ONE: **Plan!**

What steps will you take this week to help someone in need? Put some thought into your response. Don't just give some vague answer like, "I'll do something nice for someone I don't know." Be specific. What exactly are you planning to do? When will you do it? How will you use what you have to help those in need?

STEP TWO: **Do!**

If you did take some steps to help someone in need, did things progress as you thought they would? Was being selflessly generous easier or harder than you expected? What was the most difficult part of helping someone else?

STEP THREE: **Review!**

What do you think Jesus would say about your efforts to help people in need? Do you feel any different toward the people you helped? Do you think they feel any different toward you?

LITTLE BIBLE BACKGROUND

Link 2

If your students aren't familiar with the Bible, it may be a mistake to assume they know much about Jesus' sacrifice. Take a minute or two to explain (1) why Jesus came to earth in human form (Philippians 2:5-11), (2) how He took the punishment that we deserved for our sins (Hebrews 10), and (3) how His death and resurrection bridged the gap between God and humanity, making eternal life possible for those who believe in Him (John 3:16).

Link 3

Refer back to the Bible story in Link 2. Using the indifference of the priest and the Levite to the injured man's pain as a starting point, ask your group members to list some reasons why people today often choose not to help those who are in need. Help your Bible rookies see the 2000-year-old story of the good Samaritan in a modern light.

ADVANCED LEARNERS

Link 2

Briefly explore the racial and spiritual differences that separated Jewish people and Samaritans. See how many of your group members know that most Jews considered the Samaritans to be an inferior people because they were a mixed-blood race. If you have time, extend the conversation to include the racial tensions that prevent some people from showing kindness and generosity to others in today's world.

Link 3

With their accountability partners, have the students list one or two people at their school or at church they know need help. Ask, **What, if anything, keeps you from getting involved in helping them?** Ask the accountability partners to write or remember the name of their partner's person and pray for boldness for their partner for the upcoming week.

MOSTLY GUYS

Link 2

Ask your group members to name five reasons why guys in particular are reluctant to get involved in other people's problems. Chances are, at least one of your students will mention the fear of rejection or doing the wrong thing. Ask, **Why is it often hard for us to get beyond our own hang ups to be able to focus on the needs of others. What would have happened if the Samaritan from the story had only thought about himself and not the dying man?**

Link 3

For a quick diversion, work with your group members to come up with a "servant's workout." Make a list of service opportunities to the poor and needy that could also double as exercise. For example, your health-minded group members might volunteer to mow and edge a neighbor's lawn, coach a local students' basketball team, or shovel driveways on winter days. Suggest that anything that benefits your neighbors *and* increases your heart rate is a doubly effective ministry.

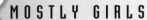

MOSTLY GIRLS
Link 2

The story of the good Samaritan raises some obvious safety issues that you may or may not want to address in this meeting. To put the matter in its simplest form, ask: **Do you think it would be a wise idea for you or your friends to follow the good Samaritan's example in today's world? Would you recommend pulling over to the side of the road to help someone who seemed to be in need?** Discuss some ways in which we can be effective helpers without putting ourselves in danger.

Link 3

Throw out this question: **Are there areas in which girls are more effective helpers than guys? If so, what are some of those areas and why?** It should be interesting to hear your group members take on this matter.

MEDIA
Link 1

Treat your group members to an oldie-but-goodie to kick off your meeting. Play the song "Help!" by The Beatles. The song can be found, appropriately enough, on the Fab Four's *Help!* album. Encourage your students to listen closely to the lyrics ("Help me if you can, I'm feeling down/And I do appreciate your being 'round"). Then, as a group, make some guesses as to what kind of help the person in the song needs. Use the tune to introduce the topic of the session.

Link 2

Show a clip of the movie *Nothing in Common,* in which Jackie Gleason and Tom Hanks play an estranged father and son. (Be sure to screen the video clip ahead of time for objectionable material.) Play the final scene of the movie, in which Jackie Gleason's character says to his son, "You're the last person I thought would come through for me." Briefly talk about the surprise of getting help from unexpected sources.

EXTRA ADRENALINE
Link 1

Kick off the meeting with a contest to see which of three contestants can be the most helpful in two minutes. When you say, **Go,** the three will do their best to assist the people in the room in any way they can. One person might go around giving ten-second backrubs. Another might straighten up the snack table. Still another might offer quick movie reviews to prevent people from wasting their money on a bad flick. At the end of the two minutes, the rest of the group should vote on who was the most helpful.

Link 2

The story of the good Samaritan is practically *begging* to be roleplayed by your group members. Imagine the fun your students will have depicting the vicious beating scene! Add to the merriment by assigning one of your students the role of the donkey who must carry the beaten traveler to the inn. Encourage your students to ham it up to get the most out of their performances.

JUNIOR HIGH

Link 2

Put your students' creativity and story-telling abilities to work by having them rewrite the parable of the good Samaritan for a modern audience. Divide the students into small groups and instruct them to retell the story as it might happen today. Your young playwrights should consider who would be the modern equivalents of the priest, the Levite, and the Samaritan. They should update the manner in which the Samaritan helps the injured man. In a nutshell, they should make any changes to the story that would make it more accessible to them and their friends. After a few minutes, have each group present its masterpiece.

Link 3

Suggest that your students start a "Good Samaritan Club" at their school. Members of this club might make a special effort to look for people in need in their classes, in the hallways, and in the lunchroom. The club could meet formally or informally to discuss and then act on the ways members can provide needed assistance. (Students who are really into the idea might even design T-shirts or some kind of accessory to identify themselves.)

Planning Checklist

LINK 1: Big Help in Small Packages
❑ Media
❑ Extra Adrenaline

LINK 2: Unexpected Mercy
❑ Little Bible Background
❑ Advanced Learners
❑ Mostly Guys
❑ Mostly Girls
❑ Media
❑ Extra Adrenaline
❑ Junior High

LINK 3: What Do You Have to Give?
❑ Little Bible Background
❑ Advanced Learners
❑ Mostly Guys
❑ Mostly Girls
❑ Junior High

WHAT A SERVANT FEELS

Key Questions

- How do our own painful experiences equip us to help others who are hurting?
- What kind of an example did Jesus set when it came to empathizing with people who are hurting?
- How can you empathize with hurting people?

Bible Base

Matthew 25:31-46
John 11:1-44
Romans 12:15

Supplies

- Flip chart
- Pens
- Pencils or pens
- Index cards
- Copies of Resources 3A, 3B, and Journal

Opener (Optional)

Common Ground

Ask your students to pull their chairs into a circle. Choose one of your group members to start the game standing in the middle of the circle. Remove his or her chair from the circle (think Musical Chairs). The person in the middle will call out a category. The category may be anything from "Collects comic books" to "Born in another state" to "Hates country music." Everyone in the group who fits the category must stand up and run to an empty seat. The person in the middle, meanwhile, must also try to get to an open chair. The person who doesn't make it must then stand in the middle of the circle and call out the next category.

MAKING IT R E A L

As you get to know your students better, pray for them specifically. Taking the time to do this will help you to focus on their needs. It will also help you to continually acknowledge and trust that it is God who is making these kids into disciples of Jesus Christ—sometimes even in spite of your efforts!

This activity may prove to be an effective bonding exercise for your group members. They may be surprised to find out that other people in the group share their interests, experiences, or background.

Link 1

Why Ask Why?

If you handed out Resource 2C at the end of Session 2, take a few minutes at the beginning of this meeting to find out how well your students did last week at giving their time and resources to people in need. Ask volunteers to share their experiences, both positive and negative, with the rest of the group. Encourage other group members to comment on the volunteers' experiences. Emphasize that you're looking for meaningful praise and suggestions. Your group members should feel comfortable enough with one another to be open and honest about their struggles and successes.

Grab your students' attention from the start by announcing that the first thing you're going to do in this session is solve some of life's most puzzling mysteries. Working in teams of three or four, your group members will attempt to answer some questions designed to make them go, "Hmmm."

LEARNER LINK

This Link activity is designed to stretch your students' brains a bit. Many of the answers on Resource 3A may sound very close to correct but are not the best answers. Watch to see how deeply your students struggle with the issue of suffering. This question has been asked through the centuries, and there is no easy answer.

It may be helpful to let your students know that you're not necessarily looking for right answers as much as you're looking for plausible answers. For the purposes of this activity, if an answer can be made to sound logical—no matter how weird it is—it's acceptable.

Read the following questions (or come up with some of your own) and give the teams a minute or so to come up with each answer.

- **Where does chalk go when it's erased?**
- **Where does snot come from?** (Or, if you prefer, **Where does nasal mucous come from?**)
- **Why do some ink pens explode?**
- **Why do certain types of music cause you to tap your feet?**

Make sure you end the activity with this question: **Why does God allow us to suffer?** To give your group members some ideas to think about, hand out copies of "There's Gotta Be a Reason" (Resource 3A). After the teams have offered their most plausible-sounding answers, focus specifically on the last reason on the sheet: "God knows that when we experience suffering, it makes us better able to help others who are suffering."

Write the word "empathy" on a flip chart and ask your students to define it. For the purposes of this session, you might settle on the following explanation: Empathy is the act of feeling what someone else is feeling, either because of a deep connection to that person or because of a shared experience, circumstance, or situation. Link 2 will introduce your students to a couple of biblical examples of empathy that meet this definition.

Link 2

Divine Empathy

Divide the group into two teams. Explain that each team will be responsible for leading a short (no longer than five minutes) study of one Bible passage. To make things easier for the teams, hand out index cards that contain (1) each team's assigned passage, (2) a few questions the team should think about, and (3) some additional Scripture references that might come in handy. Here are the assignments:

Team One: John 11:1-44
- What can we tell about the relationship between Jesus and Lazarus's family?
- Why didn't Jesus seem concerned when He was first told of Lazarus's illness?
- What do you suppose the atmosphere was like at Mary and Martha's house when Jesus arrived?
- What was it that caused Jesus to weep?
- If Jesus knew He was going to raise Lazarus from the dead, why did He weep?
- What does this passage tell us about Jesus, aside from the fact that He has power over death?
Additional references: Isaiah 53:1-12 (especially vs. 3)

Team Two: Matthew 25:31-46
- According to Jesus, how will people be divided when He judges the earth?
- Who does Jesus describe as "the least of these brothers of mine"?
- How will the "sheep" respond when Jesus rewards them?
- Why does Jesus tell the people on His left to depart from Him?
- What does this passage tell us about Jesus, aside from the fact that He will judge the world one day?
Additional references: Matthew 4:2; John 19:28; John 19:23

Allow several minutes for the teams to prepare. Give your students the freedom to be as creative as they want in presenting and explaining their passage to the rest of the group.

You may be surprised by the insights your impromptu Bible study leaders bring to the discussion. You can't, however, expect them to recognize every connection in their passage to the session topic. For that reason, you may want to refer to the following summaries to supplement your group members' understanding about Jesus' empathy.

Team One
Jesus knew that Lazarus would not be dead for long, but no one else knew that. Mary and Martha, Lazarus's sisters, and his friends and neighbors were deeply saddened by his loss. To make matters worse, Mary and Martha seemed to recognize that Jesus could have done something to save Lazarus but chose not to do so.

John 11:1-5 tells us that Jesus loved Lazarus, Mary, and Martha. When He arrived at their house and saw the pain they were in, He must have ached for them. Their hurt was His hurt, so their tears became His tears.

Team Two
Jesus has such strong feelings for the poor and downtrodden of this world that He will always notice when we help them and consider it a slap in the face when we ignore them. He wants nothing to do with people who want nothing to do with His "brothers."

But this isn't sympathy on Jesus' part; it's empathy. He wanted the hungry to be fed because He knew what it was like to be hungry. He wanted strangers to be invited in and cared for because He knew what it was like to be rejected.

After your group members have weighed in on the topic of Jesus' empathy, ask: **Maybe one of the reasons God allows us to experience pain, suffering, loss, and hard times is so that we will be better able to understand what other hurting people are going through and be better prepared to help them? Why or why not?** Let your group members offer their opinions.

Link 3

Empathy 'n' Me

Ask: **Have you ever had someone say to you, "I know just how you're feeling"? If so, how did you feel when you heard those words? Did you believe the person? Why or why not?** These words are especially popular at funerals. Usually the people who use the phrase don't mean any disrespect by it; they just might not know what else to say.

What if the person really *did* know how you feel—somewhat, at least? What if he or she had gone through a similar experience? Would you be interested in talking to that person? Why?

After a few students have offered their thoughts, say: **Okay, let's reverse the situation. Let's say you run into someone who's hurting or in need of help. Let's say that the person is going through a situation similar to one you went through a year or so ago. Would you be interested in talking to that person?** If some of your group members express reluctance, listen to their reasons for not getting involved. Invite the rest of the group to respond to those reasons.

The resource sheet "What I've Got to Give" (Resource 3B) is designed to help your group members identify the things in their lives that qualify them to be truly empathetic, the situations and circumstances they've experienced that make them experts of sorts in dealing with specific kinds of hurt. Encourage your students to take this assignment seriously. Emphasize that no one will be asked to share anything on the sheet that he or she is uncomfortable with.

After a few minutes, ask if there are any volunteers who would like to share some of the things they wrote down. After the volunteers have shared, discuss as a group the possibility that there are people in this world who can benefit from the negative things that have happened to us.

Before you wrap up this session, throw out a few more questions to the group: **What if you run into someone who's facing a problem you've never encountered? Let's say you've never had *any* experience with this kind of problem. Can you still offer that person empathy? If so, how?**

LEARNER LINK

If any of your group members are brave enough to share their responses to Resource 3B, you will need to respect their feelings, as well as their privacy. You may need to ask a few questions to clarify a point or to correct a possible misunderstanding, but try not to pry for more information. Do not put your students in a position where they feel pressure to reveal more than they want to. When your volunteers finish sharing, be quick to affirm them, and encourage the rest of the group to do the same.

MAKING IT REAL

A big part of discipleship is encouraging your students to put what they have learned into action. As their leader, you should be constantly looking for teachable moments—times when you are together with the students, outside of your group time, in which you can encourage them to practice what they have been learning. Another great way to do this is to set up service projects or experiential learning times. Session five in this book provides what you need to set up one of these learning experiences.

If your students need a hint, have someone read Romans 12:15. Then remind them of Jesus' example in John 11. Because Jesus cared so deeply for the people who were mourning Lazarus's death, He allowed their pain to become His pain. That's the model we need to learn to follow. If we truly care about the people around us, we should be able to feel their pain—at least to a certain extent.

Have students get with their accountability partners, hand out copies of the student sheet, "Heart Check: A Practical Approach to Empathy" (Resource 3C). Have each student look at the "Do It Up" section and fill out the plan for what the or she will do this week to help someone in need. Have the partners end the session with specific prayers based on their action plan for the week.

There's Gotta Be a Reason

If God loves us so much, why does He allow us to experience pain and suffering? Why doesn't He just do away with all of the hurt in our lives?

Below you'll find some answers that people have come up with as they struggled to understand why God doesn't prevent His people from suffering. Which of these reasons make sense to you? Which are too extreme to you?

1. God wants to give us a taste of what it's like to be Him. (Imagine the pain He suffered when He sacrificed His only Son to pay the price for our sins!)

2. God wants to keep us from becoming too comfortable and content in our daily lives.

3. God is powerless to stop our pain.

4. God allows us to suffer the consequences of our sin; often the result of our sin is pain and suffering.

5. God focuses His attention on one believer at a time; until it's time for Him to work in us, we must patiently endure our pain and suffering.

6. God focuses His attention on the grand scheme of the universe and stays out of the small details of our daily lives.

7. God allows us to experience pain and suffering for reasons too mysterious for us to understand.

8. God knows that when we experience suffering, it makes us better able to help others who are suffering.

What I've Got to Give

You may be surprised by how just much you have to give to hurting people. No, not just money, but life experience, the things that have happened to you—the things that have made you the person you are today. Take a look at your life. Evaluate the lessons you have learned—even if you had to learn them the hard way. Fill in the blanks below to get an idea of what you have to offer and who you can help.

Major problems I've faced in my life: _____

_____

_____

Losses I've experienced: _____

_____

_____

_____

© PhotoDisc, Inc.

Disappointments I've had to deal with: _____

_____

_____

_____

Personal struggles I've gone through: _____

_____

_____

_____

_____

Biggest mistakes I've made: _____

_____

_____

_____

_____

Here are some of the people I might be able to help because of my life experience. (For example, if your parents are divorced, you could relate to someone whose folks are thinking about splitting up.)

_____

_____

_____

Here's what I would say to someone facing a situation like mine. (You choose the situation.) If you're not sure what you would say, try it from another perspective: Here's what I wish someone had said to me when I was facing that situation.

_____

_____

_____

HEART CHECK:
A Practical Approach to Empathy

You may think you've picked up some valuable tips for empathizing with those in need, but unless you actually put them to use in your life these tips are worthless. Remember, God wants not only "listeners" of His Word, but "doers" (James 1:22). This sheet is for doers.

LOOK IT UP

Below you'll find seven Scripture references, one for every day of the week. Each passage listed below has something interesting to say about empathy for others. Spend a few minutes each day looking up the passage and writing down a few (relevant) thoughts that pop into your head.

DAY ONE: Philippians 1:29-30 (What do you think it means to "suffer" for Jesus?)

_____
_____
_____
_____

DAY TWO: Philippians 4:14 (How would you go about sharing in someone else's troubles?)

_____
_____
_____
_____

DAY THREE: 2 Corinthians 4:17-18 (How can you help other people focus on what is "unseen"?)

_____
_____
_____
_____

DAY FOUR: 2 Corinthians 11:28-29 (How do you suppose Paul was able to feel the weaknesses of others?)

_____
_____
_____

☺ TALK IT UP

Jesus tells us that "all things are possible with God" (Mark 10:27). That includes using the pain and suffering you've experienced in your own life to help others. So when you're faced with a situation that calls for you to put some of your hard-earned life lessons to use, a wise first step is to consult the One who makes all things possible. Take some time to write down a few prayer requests, specific ways in which you need the Lord to help you empathize with others. (For example, you might ask Him to help you recognize what you have to offer certain people.) Don't be afraid to get personal here. No one else needs to see your prayer request list.

_____
_____
_____
_____
_____
_____
_____
_____
_____
_____
_____
_____
_____
_____
_____
_____

DAY FIVE: Job 2:11-13 (What strikes you about the reaction of Job's three friends to Job's pain?)

_____
_____
_____
_____

DAY SIX: 2 Corinthians 1:3-4 (How does God's comfort for us affect the way we comfort others?)

_____
_____
_____
_____

DAY SEVEN: Matthew 11:28-30 (How can you assist a troubled person in finding help in Jesus?)

_____
_____
_____
_____

DO IT UP

If you're serious about following Jesus' example in empathizing with others' pain, you'll need an action plan. Take some time to answer the following questions.

STEP ONE: **Plan!**

How will you prepare yourself this week so that you're ready to help someone in need if you're given an opportunity? Put some thought into your response. Don't just settle for an easy answer. Be specific. What exactly are you planning to do? What kind of person would most benefit from your experiences? How will you go about making contact with such a person?

STEP5 TWO: **Do!**

If you did attempt to show empathy to someone in need, did it go as you had planned? What did you end up doing? Was it easier or harder than you expected? How did the person respond?

STEP THREE: **Review!**

Do you think you handled the situation in a way Jesus might have handled it? If you had the opportunity to do it over again, what would you do differently? Do you feel any different toward the person now? Do you think he or she feels any different toward you?

LITTLE BIBLE BACKGROUND
Link 1

If your group members aren't familiar with what the Bible says about God, Resource 3A may raise more questions than it answers. If possible, go through the following Scripture passages to address some of the false claims about God on Resource 3A: (1) John 3:16; (2) Philippians 4:11-13; (3) Matthew 19:26; (4) Romans 5:12-21; (5) Psalm 33:13-15; (7) Isaiah 55:9.

Link 2

Needed: candy bar

If you're looking for a relatively quick diversion for your Bible rookies, offer a candy bar or some other incentive to the first person who can memorize John 11:35 ("Jesus wept"). Make sure your group members keep their Bibles closed until you give a signal. You might announce that the first person to find the verse, memorize it, stand up, and recite it will be declared the winner.

ADVANCED LEARNERS
Link 1

If you don't think your group members are challenged enough by your discussion of empathy, throw out a few really tough questions. Ask: **Why do you suppose God chooses to work through painful situations? Why doesn't He just work through happiness or laughter? What might He find useful about suffering?**

Link 3

Spend a few minutes concentrating on the nuts and bolts of empathy. Ask: **How would you try to convince someone who's hurting that you kind of know how it feels? What things would you say or not say to show your empathy?** If you really want to get deeper with this discussion, you could have group members predict how hurting people might respond to different approaches.

MOSTLY GUYS
Link 2

Say: **True or false? If you're not naturally empathetic toward people who are hurting, it's because you're self-centered.** Ideally, this question will lead to a mini-debate over whether some people are more naturally empathetic than others. Some claim it's a gender issue, that girls are more likely to be empathetic than guys. What do your group members think?

Link 3

If your guys put more stock in common sense and practicality than in emotional bonding, ask, **What kind of things can you do with the painful experiences of your past?** To supplement their answers, point out that there are really three things you can do with the pains of the past. One, you can be angry about them and constantly look for revenge. Two, you can try to forget about them and bury your feelings. Three, you can come to grips with them and use what you learned from them to help others. The key point is this: Don't let your pain go to waste.

MOSTLY GIRLS

Link 2

Say: **True or false? The more emotional you are by nature, the more empathy you will feel for hurting people.** Ideally, this question will lead to an interesting discussion on the difference between emotions (like sympathy, for example) and empathy. Some people claim that sympathy is condescending, while empathy is an effort to find common ground. What do your group members think?

Link 3

Ask: **How well do you have to know or understand someone before you can empathize with them? For example, do you think it's harder to empathize with guys than it is with other girls? If so, why do you think that is?** Briefly discuss some ideas for increasing your group members' empathy toward the opposite sex.

MEDIA

Link 1

Bring in clips of the TV show "America's Funniest Videos" (or any similar program). Play some scenes of people falling down, getting hit with flying objects, or any other (mildly) painful situation. Watch for your group members to cringe when they see painful things happen in the clips. Use their reactions to introduce the topic empathy, feeling what other people are feeling.

Link 3

Bring in some articles from your local newspaper that deal with recent tragedies in your area. Hand out the articles and ask students to read them aloud. After each article is read, ask your group members to rate each incident on a scale of one to ten, based on how tragic they consider it. You will likely see some of your group members "empathy biases" come to the surface. For example, someone who's lost a sibling may empathize strongly with a story about a teenager killed by a drunk driver.

EXTRA ADRENALINE

Link 1

If you don't think your students would appreciate the brainy aspects of the activity in Link 1, try an activity called "Mirror" instead. You'll need two volunteers, who will stand facing each other. One person will start making movements, and the other will try to "mirror" or copy them. You can have a lot of fun with this game if you can get your group members to commit to it wholeheartedly. Use this activity to introduce the idea of common experiences and empathy.

Link 3

Challenge your action-oriented students to busy themselves with the work of empathy. To practice, have pairs silently roleplay 15-second vignettes of helping someone in need. Ask, **How many of these vignettes were realistic? What did you learn from them?** Encourage them to find one person at school or in their neighborhood who's struggling with loneliness or disconnectedness, and begin an empathetic relationship with him or her. You might even encourage your group members to invite their new acquaintances to an upcoming church event.

JUNIOR HIGH

Link 1

If you think the tough-question activity in Link 1 may be beyond your junior highers' capabilities, try an alternative called "Who Am I?" You will read a series of first-person descriptions and students will guess who you are. Ideally you should use descriptions of people or characters your students are familiar with. Here are a couple of examples to get you started:

• **After I get off work from my newspaper job, I like to cruise around the city of Metropolis, looking for trouble.** (Clark Kent/Superman)

• **Just like my jersey—number 23—I'm retired now. But that doesn't mean I'm too old to whip you in a game of one-on-one.** (Michael Jordan)

For maximum effect, come up with a description only the people in your group would know, perhaps of a volunteer worker or even the pet of one of your group members ("Yesterday was a good day. I chased three squirrels out of the yard, buried two bones, and tore up one of Gary's new shoes").

This game will give your students some practice in identifying the things that are going on in people's lives—the same principles that are involved in empathy.

Link 2

Rather than asking your junior highers to lead a Bible study, recruit them as Bible "interpreters." As you read each passage, have your students act out the scenes being described. Assign roles according to the number of students in your group. If you have a large group, make plenty of room for extras.

Planning Checklist

LINK 1: Why Ask Why?
❏ Little Bible Background
❏ Advanced Learners
❏ Mostly Girls
❏ Media
❏ Extra Adrenaline
❏ Junior High

LINK 2: Divine Empathy
❏ Little Bible Background
❏ Mostly Guys
❏ Junior High

LINK 3: Empathy 'n' Me
❏ Advanced Learners
❏ Mostly Guys
❏ Mostly Girls
❏ Media
❏ Extra Adrenaline

WHAT A SERVANT DOES

Key Questions
• What is an extreme Christian?
• What kind of examples did Jesus set when it came to going beyond one's comfort level to serve God and others?
• How can you venture beyond your comfort zone to help someone in need?

Bible Base
Matthew 14:22-33; 26:6-13, 36-44

Supplies:
• Soap and water (optional)
• Baker's chocolate, melted candy bar, chocolate chip cookie, chocolate syrup (optional)
• Pencils or pens
• Copies of Resources 4A, 4B, and Journal

Opener (Optional)
Prove Your Love
Warning: this activity can get messy—really messy. You'll need to make sure you have some soap, water, and other miscellaneous cleaning supplies available.

Start things off by asking: **How many of you love chocolate?** Most hands will probably shoot up pretty quickly. Clarify the question a bit: **How many of you really, *really* love chocolate?** Some of your more cautious group members may sense that something's up and put their hands down.

LEARNER **LINK**

Jesus always sets for us the most extreme example. He went out of His comfort zone—heaven—to take on human form and live on earth. Ultimately, it was His unwavering devotion to following God that led Him to endure the physical pain and emotional shame of the cross. Jesus is, in all ways, our most extreme example of a disciple of God.

MAKING IT REAL

One of the benefits of leading a small discipleship group is the chance to reach out to some of the parents and families of the students. Make a point, any chance you get, to talk with them and to let them know what you have been doing in your group. Parents appreciate that, and it can help them encourage their students at home. Not all of the parents may be Christians, so be aware that they are looking for the characteristics of Jesus in your life.

How many of you would be willing to prove how much you love chocolate? Choose three people with their hands raised to prove their love in front of the rest of the group.

The "proving methods" you use will depend on the supplies you can get your hands on. Here are some ideas to get you started:
• Which of your contestants would be willing to eat baking chocolate?
• Which of your contestants would be willing to eat a melted candy bar without using their hands?
• Which of your contestants would be willing to sing a love song to a chocolate chip cookie?
• Which of your contestants would be willing to wash their hair with chocolate syrup?

Each test should be a little more distasteful than the one before it. If one of your volunteers refuses a test, he or she is out. Continue until only one person remains. Declare him or her to be the most extreme chocolate lover in your group.

Then ask: **What if we were looking for the most extremely committed disciple in the group? What kind of tests might we conduct?** Get a few responses before moving on to Link 1.

Link 1

I Can't Believe I Did That!

If you handed out Resource 3C at the end of Session 3, take a few minutes at the beginning of this meeting to find out how your students' attempts at empathizing with someone in pain went. Ask volunteers to share their experiences, both positive and negative, with the rest of the group. Encourage other group members to comment on the volunteers' experiences. Emphasize that you're looking for meaningful praise and suggestions. Your group members should feel comfortable enough with each other to be open and honest about their struggles and successes.

Hand out copies of "Extremes" (Resource 4A). Give your students a few minutes to fill out the sheet. When they're finished, briefly discuss some of their responses. Do not, however, spend a lot of time on the sheet. Its purpose is merely to introduce the idea of extremes and lead up to this question: **What's the most extreme thing you've ever done as a Christian?** For some people, it might be attending a youth group retreat. For others, it might be sharing their faith with a stranger. For others, it might be traveling to a foreign country to build houses for the poor. Value all answers given.

Then ask: **Who set the most extreme example in the Bible? Let's take a look at what Jesus did to make Him so extreme in obedience and service.**

Link 2

Not My Will . . .

Have your group members open their Bibles to Matthew 26:36-44. Explain that while you read the passage aloud, your students should follow along in their Bibles to make sure that you don't misread something or leave any parts out. Read the following "adaptation" of the passage, pausing at the ellipses to give your students a chance to correct you.

Then Jesus went with his disciples to a place called Gethsemane, and he said to them, "Sit here while I go over there and pray." He took Peter and the two sons of Zebedee along with him, and Jesus was very happy . . .

Oh, you're right, Jesus wasn't happy, but deeply troubled. Continue, **And [Jesus] began to be sorrowful and troubled. Then he said to them, "My soul is overwhelmed with sorrow, even to the point of death. Stay here and keep watch with me." Going a little farther, he fell with his face to the ground and prayed, "My Father, if it is possible, may this cup be taken from me. But no matter what you say, I'm not going to die tomorrow. . . ."** Okay, that's not quite what happened. What did Jesus say? Have the students read the last part of vs. 29.

Continue, **Then he returned to the disciples and found them sleeping. "Could you not keep watch with me for one hour?" he asked Peter. "Watch and pray so that you will not fall into temptation. The spirit is weak but the body is strong. . . . "** You caught me. But what do you think Jesus meant by saying, "The spirit is willing but the body is weak?"

Continue, **He went away a second time and prayed, "My Father, if it is not possible for this cup to be taken away unless I drink it, I might do what you ask when the time comes, if I feel like it."** Pause.

Ask rhetorically, **Have any of you ever prayed something like this to God?**
Continue, **When he came back, he again found them sleeping because they were tired. So he left them and went away once more, praying about something completely different. . . . Okay, that's not true either. Why did Jesus pray about the same thing for a third time?**

When you finish reading the passage, ask: **What happened to Jesus in the 24 hours after this story?** (He was tried, sentenced, and executed by crucifixion.) **How does knowing this shed some light on Jesus' words and actions in the garden of Gethsemane?**

Jesus paid the ultimate price in obedience and devotion to God: He gave up His life to follow God's plan. And while that may sound incredibly intimidating to you, let's look at other ways people around Jesus showed their devotion and obedience to Him. Hand out copies of "Biblical Extremists" (Resource 4B). Let the group members work in pairs to complete the sheet. Use the following comments to supplement their answers as you discuss the two Bible stories.

A Late Night Stroll (Matthew 14:22-33)
• Peter may have been motivated by an overwhelming desire to be with the Lord. He saw Jesus walking on the water and wanted to join Him. He trusted Jesus to take care of the details.
• The disciples were just regular guys, so they were probably as freaked out by Peter's bold move as we would be under the same conditions.
• It's possible that Peter could have drowned when he went overboard, so it's probably safe to say he risked his life to show his love for Jesus. He certainly risked his safety by leaving the boat. He also risked his reputation among the rest of the disciples. Who knows? They may have made fun of him for his lack of faith once he got onto the water.
• The fact that Jesus allowed Peter to walk on top of the water with Him suggests that He was pleased with Peter's boldness. The fact that He was quick to come to the rescue when Peter began sinking seems to indicate that He protects those who take chances for His sake.

The Sweet Smell of Discipleship (Matthew 26:6-13)
• This may have been the woman's only opportunity to show the Lord in person how much she loved Him. The price of the perfume meant nothing. The opportunity to honor Jesus meant everything.
• It's possible that the woman felt a little self-conscious and embarrassed when the disciples started objecting to her actions. Maybe she even questioned herself, figuring the disciples knew more than she did about how she should express her love for the Lord.
• Obviously the woman risked the possibility of wasting a very expensive possession. She also risked public humiliation. No one seemed to understand why she would do such a thing.
• Jesus strongly defended the woman's actions. He made everyone in the room recognize that what she did with the perfume was much more meaningful than anything else she could have done.

After you've gone through the sheet, ask: **What do these stories have in common?** Work with your group members to come up with a list of common themes from the Bible accounts. Ask, **Does the word "extreme" work here to describe the stories? Why?** (The stories all involve some kind of risk. They all involve some pretty extreme actions. They all involve a person moving beyond his or her "comfort zone.") **How was Jesus the ultimate model of extreme giving for these people? For us today?**

The Comfort Zone and Beyond

Ask: **Do you think you have it in you to do something extreme for Jesus like Peter or the woman with the perfume?** Encourage your students to put some thought into their answers and to explain why they think they are or aren't capable of such acts.

When you think of "extreme discipleship," what images pop into your head? What kinds of things might an extreme disciple do in today's world? Some of your students may mention going overseas to be a missionary or giving away large amounts of money.

Point out that it's difficult to come up with one all-encompassing description of an "extreme" disciple because what's *extreme* for one person may be normal—or impossible—for another. Sometimes it's the place we live, or limitations with our bodies, that keep us from risking things that others can. But that doesn't mean that some are called to give while others can just "sit on the sidelines."

Say: **The key to extreme discipleship is moving beyond our comfort zone.** Suggest to your group members that most people have pretty predictable habits, routines, and tendencies. We feel comfortable hanging out with the same people, going to the same church, and participating in the same youth group activities. Moving beyond those natural boundaries requires a little risk on our part.

Remind your students of the extreme example Jesus set. Ask, **Does Jesus ever ask us to do something He hasn't already done? Does He understand your feelings of fear and uncertainty that come with risk? How do you know?**

LEARNER LINK

Remind your students that they may not ever be asked to die for their faith. The key, however, is for your students to get that, while it may not exactly matter what they do, they should do something. Jesus wants us to move beyond the safety of our four-walled life into something extreme. It may start slowly, but the less we are bogged down by "safe" things, the more responsive we can be to Jesus' extreme call.

MAKING IT REAL

Don't give your students the impression that it's easy to follow Jesus' example! If you don't acknowledge the challenges, some of your group members may leave with unrealistic expectations. Prepare your students for these unfortunate possibilities by talking honestly about how people may respond to them and risks that are involved in being a disciple of Jesus Christ. Rather than discouraging your group members, you may find that your straightforward approach actually motivates many of them.

Ask: **How "extreme" would you be willing to go as a disciple of Jesus? For example—**
• **Would you be willing to risk rejection by sharing Jesus' love with another person?**
• **Would you be willing to risk the unpopularity that might result from hanging out with someone other people find undesirable?**
• **Would you be willing to give up some of your free time to help people who need you?**
• **Would you be willing to give a certain percentage of the money you earn to help less fortunate people?**
• **Would you be willing to risk being laughed at and mocked for taking a public stand for Jesus?**
Ask your students to suggest any other examples of extreme discipleship they can think of before they start answering these questions.

Rather than discuss these questions as a group, give your students a chance to talk to the Lord about them. Set aside a few minutes at the end of your session so your students can fill out the "Do It Up" portion of "Heart Check: A Practical Approach to Extreme Discipleship" (Resource 4C). To close, allow your students a few minutes for silent prayer. Let your students seek wisdom from God about their relationship with Him and perhaps commit themselves to more "extreme" acts of discipleship.

Extremes

Does your life feel like a contradiction? At one time boring and predictable, at another time wild and uncontrolled? What's . . .

©PhotoDisc, Inc.

● the scariest movie you've ever seen?

● the most boring day you've ever spent?

● the biggest risk you've ever taken?

● the closest you've come to falling asleep in class?

● the wildest hobby you've ever gotten into?

● the most dangerous career you've ever considered pursuing?

● the dumbest thing you've ever said?

Biblical **Extremists**

You wouldn't believe what some people in the Bible did to serve Jesus and follow His example. Talk about extreme discipleship! See for yourself. Look up the passages listed below and answer the questions that follow. Your answers may just put some ideas in your head—some extreme ideas.

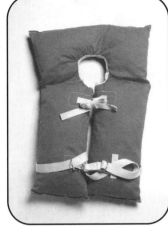

A Late Night Stroll
Matthew 14:22-33

- What do you think made Peter want to hop out of the boat in the middle of the lake?

- How do you think the other disciples responded when they saw what Peter was going to do?

- What did Peter risk in his bold effort to follow Jesus?

- What can we tell about Jesus' reaction to Peter's extreme move?

The Sweet Smell of Discipleship
Matthew 26:6-13

- Why do you suppose the woman chose to honor Jesus in such an expensive way?

- How do you think the reaction of Jesus' disciples might have made her feel?

- What did the woman risk in her unusual offering?

- What can we tell about Jesus' reaction to the woman's deed?

HEART CHECK:
A Practical Approach to Extreme Discipleship

You may think you've picked up some valuable tips for going beyond your comfort zone at today's meeting, but unless you actually put them to use in your life these tips are worthless. Remember, God wants not only "listeners" of His Word, but "doers" (James 1:22). This sheet is for doers.

LOOK IT UP

Below you'll find seven Scripture references, one for every day of the week. Each passage listed below has something interesting to say about extreme discipleship. Spend a few minutes each day looking up the passage and writing down a few (relevant) thoughts that pop into your head.

DAY ONE: Mark 1:16-20 (What did the disciples leave behind to follow Jesus?)

_____
_____
_____
_____

DAY TWO: Matthew 10:1-20 (How do you think the disciples felt about starting a road trip with no money or any other provisions?)

_____
_____
_____

DAY THREE: Luke 7:36-50 (What did the woman risk to show her love for Jesus?)

_____
_____
_____

DAY FOUR: Mark 10:29-31 (What does this passage tell us about the sacrifices we make for Jesus?)

_____
_____
_____
_____

☺ TALK IT UP

Jesus tells us that "all things are possible with God" (Mark 10:27). That includes extreme discipleship. So when we're faced with a really difficult situation, with doing something we've never done before, a wise first step is to consult the One who makes all things possible. Take some time to write down a few prayer requests, specific ways in which you need the Lord to help you. (For example, you might ask Him to give you strength and courage when you venture beyond your comfort zone.) Don't be afraid to get personal here. No one else needs to see your prayer request list.

_____
_____
_____
_____
_____
_____
_____
_____
_____
_____
_____
_____
_____
_____
_____
_____
_____
_____
_____

DAY FIVE: Luke 18:18-25 (What are some things you would have a hard time giving up?)

_____

_____

_____

_____

DAY SIX: Genesis 22:1-18 (How do you think Isaac felt about being sacrificed by his father?)

_____

_____

_____

_____

DAY SEVEN: John 15:13 (Who or what would you be willing to give your life for?)

_____

_____

_____

_____

DO IT UP

If you're serious about following the biblical examples of gutsy discipleship, you'll need a plan of action. Here's a three-step plan designed just for you. Take some time to answer the following questions.

STEP ONE: **Plan!**

What are you going to do this week to step beyond your comfort zone? Put some thought into your response. Be specific. What exactly are you planning to do? When will you do it? How will you deal with people's reactions?

STEP TWO: **Do!**

If you took the plunge and crossed over into uncharted discipleship territory, did it go as you had planned? What did you end up doing? How did you feel right before you made your move? Was it easier or harder than you expected?

STEP THREE: **Review!**

Do you think you handled the situation in a way that Jesus might appreciate? If you had a chance to do it over again, what would you do differently?

LITTLE BIBLE BACKGROUND

Link 1

It may be presumptuous to assume that all, or even most, of your students are Christians. For that reason, you may want to reword the question, **What's the most extreme thing you've ever done as a Christian?** Instead, ask your group members: **What's the most outrageous or surprising thing anyone has ever done to help you?** After several students have shared their answers, turn the question around. Ask: **What's the most extreme thing you've ever done to help someone else?**

Link 2

Help your group members understand that Jesus appreciated the risky actions of Peter and the woman with perfume because He Himself was no stranger to risk. Have someone read John 10:22-39 and John 11:1-16. Point out that Jesus was not afraid to enter hostile territory, even if it meant His life was in danger. He was committed to God's work, and nothing was going to stand in His way.

ADVANCED LEARNERS

Link 2

If you really want to challenge your students in the area of extreme discipleship, throw Jesus' advice to the rich young man in Mark 10:21 at them: "Go, sell everything you have and give it to the poor, and you will have treasure in heaven. Then come, follow me." Ask: **Should we take Jesus' words literally? Is that really the kind of extreme commitment it takes to follow Him?** Briefly discuss whether you should start advertising all of your possessions in the "For Sale" section of the newspaper.

Link 3

Ask your group members to do some self-reflection and describe their "comfort zones." Encourage them to consider as many different aspects of their Christian life as possible. For example, under what circumstances, if any, are they comfortable talking about how they became a Christian? What kind of people are they comfortable helping? How much time are they comfortable spending on "Christian things"?

MOSTLY GUYS

Link 2

Say: **Put yourself in the sandals of the paralyzed man's four friends. How far would you have been willing to go to help your disabled buddy? Would you have carried him to see Jesus in the first place? Would you have turned around when you saw the crowd? Would you have been willing to destroy someone's roof in the process? Be honest.** Briefly discuss how far is far enough when it comes to helping a friend.

Link 3

Ask someone from your group or your church who's an experienced skydiver to talk about the first time he or she stood in the doorway of a plane, getting ready to jump. Compare the nervousness of that experience with the apprehension of leaving one's comfort zone. Point out that while it may be hard to take that first leap of faith, after you do it the first time, it becomes much easier and much less scary.

MOSTLY GIRLS

Link 2

Ask your group members to make a list of the reasons comfort zones are so difficult to break out of. Your students may come up with suggestions like "It's best to stick with what you know" and "If you fail miserably, you may ruin your reputation and your credibility." If you have time at the end of your meeting, go back through the list and address each reason individually. Discuss why we shouldn't allow that reason to prevent us from expanding our discipleship into new and deeper areas.

Link 3

Ask one of the female leaders of your church to talk briefly to your group about some of the obstacles and opportunities she's faced in her ministry. Ask her to talk specifically about how she prepared herself to step beyond her comfort zone and what happened when she finally did. Use her story as an example/cautionary tale for your group members.

MEDIA

Link 1

Looking for a bang-up way to introduce the concept of extremism? Show some clips of "The World's Scariest Police Chases" or any other reality-based TV program that captures people in extreme situations. Talk briefly about the risks involved in each scene before moving on to a discussion of the risks involved in extreme discipleship.

Link 3

Play the song "What If I Stumble" by dc Talk, which deals with the fear of moving beyond one's comfort zone. Focus specifically on lyrics like "What if I stumble, what if I fall? What if I lose my step and make fools of us all?" Ask, **Why do questions like this hold us back from risk?**

EXTRA ADRENALINE

Link 1

Needed: Sports equipment

Any game can be made "extreme" with just a few modifications. For example, regular old dodgeball becomes Extreme Dodgeball when you play with seven balls instead of one. Volleyball, likewise, becomes Extreme Volleyball when your students are trying to keep two or three balls going at the same time. Kick off the meeting with an extreme version of one of your students' favorite games.

Link 2

Needed: Plastic containers, spoons, water bucket

Divide your group into two teams. Give each team a small plastic container and a spoon. Place a bucket of water at one end of the yard or room. Each team will start from the line, run across the yard, fill their container, one spoonful per person, with the "perfume" (water) until it is full. Then, they will run and pour the "perfume" on your feet. The first team to complete this wins.

JUNIOR HIGH
Link 1

Before you "officially" begin the meeting, ask two group members to run an errand for you. It doesn't matter what the errand is, as long as it's complicated, time-consuming, and requires a lot of work. For example, you might say: **I need the two of you to change the right front tire of my car. When you're finished, take the old tire to Pastor Smith's car on the other side of the church. He said he could fix it for me. Then go to Pastor Smith's office and ask him if we can borrow a few of the church's old hymnals. I think they're stored in the basement. I just hope the rats haven't gotten to them. He'll tell you where they are and what you'll have to dig through to get to them. When you find them, bring back three of them.** Watch your volunteers' faces as you spell out the details of the errand. See how anxious they are to leave the comfort zone of your meeting room when they find out all that you want them to do.

Link 3

Your junior highers may not have had time to settle into a "comfort zone," as far as their Christian life is concerned. So rather than encouraging them to step out of such a zone, spend some time as a group brainstorming some ways your students can emulate the biblical examples in Link 2. Ask your group members to name some areas in which they could be doing more as a disciple. Then come up with some workable ideas for expanding the scope of their discipleship.

Planning Checklist

LINK 1: I Can't Believe I Did That!
❑ Little Bible Background
❑ Media
❑ Extra Adrenaline
❑ Junior High

LINK 2: Not My Will . . .
❑ Little Bible Background
❑ Advanced Learners
❑ Mostly Guys
❑ Mostly Girls
❑ Extra Adrenaline

LINK 3: The Comfort Zone and Beyond
❑ Advanced Learners
❑ Mostly Guys
❑ Mostly Girls
❑ Media
❑ Junior High

REALITY CHECK: SERVANTS IN ACTION

About This Session

This bonus session is designed to help your group members understand discipleship in a deeper, more hands-on way. During the four sessions of this book, you are talking about what it means to adopt the values of Jesus. True discipleship involves the heart, the head, and the hands. During this session you'll give your kids a chance to take the things that they are learning and experiencing and put them into practice in the real world. This experiential learning time is a good way to wrap up your four weeks of study, but it can also be done at any point throughout the study.

Check It Out

For this session we recommend that you and your group visit a local nursing home. You will find that the residents of the home are extremely receptive to visitors and are very appreciative of any efforts you make on their behalf. This is especially important if your group members have little experience in on-site ministry. Of course, make sure that you work with the nursing home staff ahead of time to coordinate your visit.

A great way to spend time with people and show them they are valued would be to instruct your group members to mingle with the nursing home residents—talking and listening to them, meeting their need for companionship. Your hope, of course, is that your kids will begin relationships with people in the home that will be sustained long after your group's visit.

If at all possible, plan your trip so that you're able to spend at least a full hour with the people you're visiting. Any less than that, and your trip will feel rushed—and the last thing you want to do is give the impression that you're in a hurry to leave.

Take It Deeper

Your students might want to put some of their talents and experiences in performing to good use. One option would be to present a mini-program at the elderly care center, with each member of your group responsible for one part of the program. For example, one person might be in charge of leading the group in prayer. Another might be in charge of finding an appropriate Scripture passage to read and comment on. Another might be responsible for finding or organizing music for the program. Still another might be in charge of making or buying small, but meaningful, gifts to hand out to the residents. Make sure each of your kids has a task that he or she is comfortable with.

Think It Through

Ideally you will spend most of your debriefing time listening to your group members' experiences in the "real world." Encourage your kids to share their feelings about helping people they don't know. If you need some discussion guides, use any or all of the following questions.

• Based on your experience today, how good would you say you are at giving of yourself? In what areas do you need improvement?

• Was your experience what you expected it to be? If so, what did you expect? If not, how was it different? Were you pleasantly surprised or a little disappointed? Explain.

• How appreciative were the people you talked to? Did they seem genuinely pleased to see you? Did any of them seem bothered or irritated by your efforts to help? How did their reactions affect your attitude?

• What's the most important thing you learned from your experience today?

• How likely is it that you will do something similar to what you did today when you're by yourself? Explain.

As you wrap up the discussion, remind your group members that the key to giving of ourselves is to remind ourselves that we're actually doing it for Jesus.

Close the meeting (and this study) with prayer. Thank God for your group members and their willingness to commit themselves to discipleship, and the hard work and unselfishness that it requires. Ask God to help your kids follow Christ's example of giving of Himself to help needy and hurting people.

Name	Address	Phone	Parent Names	e-mail	B-day	Notes
1.						
2.						
3.						
4.						
5.						
6.						
7.						
8.						
9.						
10.						
11.						
12.						
13.						
14.						
15.						

Lift IT UP

Ephesians 3:16-19 "I pray that out of his glorious riches he may strengthen you with power through his Spirit in your inner being, so that Christ may dwell in your hearts through faith. And I pray that you, being rooted and established in love, may have power, together with all the saints, to grasp how wide and long and high and deep is the love of Christ, and to know this love that surpasses knowledge—that you may be filled to the measure of all the fullness of God."

Learn how you can teach your teens to build rock-solid relationships with each other and with Jesus.

BRING 'EM BACK ALIVE is a unique, 12-book study series that shows the all-too-human side of major Bible figures—and how God used them greatly. Each book contains 5 sections . . . focusing on characters like Peter, David, and Ruth.

NEW!

CUSTOM DISCIPLESHIP takes a step beyond asking *"What Would Jesus Do?"* This 16-title series equips kids with the answers— they'll find out exactly what Jesus did in all kinds of relevant everyday situations, covering topics like measuring success, loving God's Word, and giving.

CUSTOM CURRICULUM effectively reaches teens with proven programs that encourage and challenge them. More than 30 titles let you choose from over 150 options. Great for small groups and large groups. They fit within short meeting times or long. You can spend more time on worship, fellowship, or study. And the materials work for seasoned Christian kids as well as the unchurched.

Choose from Junior High/Middle School titles or the High School series.

QUICK STUDIES inspire genuine self-discovery through Old & New Testament Bible studies. They're extremely relevant to the issues faced by teenagers, and they're interactive–using games, surveys, and case studies to make kids think and open up. More than 40 sessions/title, 10 titles in all.

To order now
Call 1-800-323-7543
In Canada, call 1-800-263-2664